POLITICAL JUSTICE

A POEM

(ANONYMOUS)

(1736)

THE AUGUSTAN REPRINT SOCIETY

PUBLICATION NUMBER 111

1965

The Augustan Reprint Society

POLITICAL JUSTICE.
A POEM.

(ANONYMOUS. 1736)

INTRODUCTION
BY
BURTON R. POLLIN AND JOHN W. WILKES

PUBLICATION NUMBER III

WILLIAM ANDREWS CLARK MEMORIAL LIBRARY

UNIVERSITY OF CALIFORNIA, LOS ANGELES

1965

2-7

INTRODUCTION

An interesting chain of events led one of the editors to search for *Political Justice.* Glancing through the pages of the *Gentleman's Magazine* for April, 1736, he amusedly noted a laudatory review of the work, borrowed from *Fog's Weekly Journal* of April 17. There was a striking similarity to William Godwin's major work of 1793 in the title and in a few of the key ideas in the excerpts printed. Yale University yielded a fine copy, purchased in 1927; subsequently another appeared in the British Museum, acquired in 1956, and a third in the William Andrews Clark Memorial Library, purchased in 1941. (The last is now being reprinted.) Thus far the editors have found the work in no other collection. Its rarity might therefore explain the total absence of any comment since its publication, save for three contemporary notices.[1] The *London Magazine* dismisses it in a sentence, while the *Gentleman's* gives an almost verbatim transcription of the review in *Fog's Journal.* This is a full page summary interspersed with several lengthy quotations and concluding with an approving reference to the poem's "encomium upon those young Patriots who have lately appeared upon the Scene of Business, and are the Glory and Honour of the present Age."[2] Obviously both journals favored the anti-Walpole group, known as Cobham's Cubs or Cousinhood. The partiality of *Fog's Journal* is not surprising since George Lyttelton, a central member of the group, has been identified as regularly contributing with Lord Chesterfield to *Common Sense,* the 1737 successor to *Fog's.*[3] We shall attempt to evaluate the purely poetic and philosophic merit of this political poem after considering its historical background.

The English political scene from 1720 to 1740 was dominated by the personality of Sir Robert Walpole. Having risen to power during the South Sea Bubble, Walpole proceeded to entrench himself by carefully playing the politicians against each other. When any one opponent was sufficiently isolated, Sir Robert would find an excuse to remove him from office. Thus by 1730 with the resignation of Viscount Townshend, the Walpole government faced a completely fragmented and disorganized opposition with Sir Robert directing all aspects of the ministry. Moreover, the essential political unit of the eighteenth century was established in the small groups of men centered around a personal friend and leader.

The personal nature of eighteenth century politics is certainly an outstanding characteristic. In addition, the small number of those politically qualified and articulate made politics the occupation of an élite, which shared a common background of wealth, education, customs, and traditions. These factors often tended to make their political activities vitriolic and even vicious; thus the intense pamphlet warfare of the age. Government and opposition groups hired professional writers to produce propaganda, the patron always being shown as correct and virtuous and the enemy politicians as venal and wicked. No charge or innuendo was too vile to be used, although usually behind the safeguard of anonymity. Occasionally even the leading figures dipped their pens into ink for a personal diatribe. On rare occasions a politician would change his tactics and write an appeal for calm reasonableness. The pamphlet, broadside, or poem might denounce corruption and demand a return to "good English political practice." These were seldom of high literary or theoretical value, being intended to promote the prestige of the author or his patron. Often they are a written reflection of public speeches.

Into this political world came Philip Yorke in 1720 when he was appointed Solicitor-General. In the reorganization of the ministry in 1724 he was promoted to Attorney-General. For nine years he filled this position with serious attention to, and respect for, the common law. By 1733 his legal ability, personal reputation, and friendship with the Duke of Newcastle made him a logical candidate for one of the two top legal offices of the country, both of which were vacant. On October 31, 1733, Yorke was made Chief Justice of the King's Bench and on November 24 Baron Hardwicke of Hardwicke in Gloucestershire. It was while he occupied this post that *Political Justice* appeared, addressed to him. From 1737 to 1762 he served as Lord Chancellor of Great Britain.

Clearly, someone out of office is aiming to flatter a ministerial

figure of popular esteem through a political poem. Although Hard-
wicke's personal reputation for legal skill and strict justice was
never seriously questioned during the forty years of his major of-
fices, in later life he was frequently attacked by opposition politi-
cians as being greedy for money, sinecures, and other advantages
for his family. Both praise and attack were true; Hardwicke,
like most men, had a mixture of qualities. In 1736, however,
he still was above the political fray. He was not yet distincly
identified with Walpole and Newcastle, and their opponents
regarded him as a possible recruit to their forces. The poem pre-
sents a clear example of the political contest on a high level in its
appeal to virtue and enlightened patriotism. That last word meant
many things. Thus the monarch and the members of government
should all be "patriotic" in their aims. William Pitt, George Gren-
ville, George Lyttelton, and their friends unquestionably intended
such a meaning in their public statements, but also used it conven-
iently in the 1730's to further their own careers. Again the personal
nature of Augustan politics is obvious.

One of the major distinctions of this poem lies in its clear
presentation of enlightened principles through the discussion of
the virtues of the man addressed. Perhaps a brief outline of its
content will clarify a few points in our analysis. The poet warns
Hardwicke against falling from his eminence in morality, like so
many others in the judicial system (pp. 3-4), and counsels the use
of reason and justice, basic to order in the universe (4-5) and to
"social love" (7) and happiness (8). He denies the Mandevillian
basis of self-interest in favor of primal sociability. The next sec-
tion pointedly premises the Platonic forms as establishing a just
order of creation for the state of nature and refers to the traditional
concept of the "chain of being" (8-10). Sin, however, has broken
the "sacred union," and smothered the soul of man.[4] Law and
government now appear to counterbalance the disorder introduced
into the state of nature and redress the abusive power of property.
Yet the right of each man to his fair share is not abrogated by any
"invalid" consent (10-12) — a decidedly novel view of rights for an
Augustan, aristocratic poem.[5] Apparently sages first administered
simple laws, acting in a kind of Platonic republic, but the power

of property, basically "fraud" and "lawless force" (14) has led to
the need for complicated government, including kings and magis-
trates (12-14). The rich should regard themselves as stewards of
the poor, having stolen their all, and judges should be, like Hard-
wicke, merciful and just. Laws should be rendered rational for a
mankind which is basically so; neither the tyrannical prince nor
the mob can subvert justice for the innocent or the rational — at
least in the eyes of heaven (15-19). Spain is an unhappy example
of a nation in which "grov'ling Slaves the Royal Fiend ador'd"
(20).[6] But the young patriots of the British Parliament, Cobham's
group, will help to maintain or restore England's simple purity of
morals and government with Hardwicke, "the godlike Cato of the
youthful Race" (22-24).

It is clear that Hardwicke is used chiefly as a convenient cue
to the presentation of fairly atypical principles. Only in his being
"severely just and piously severe" and sharing the "pain" of judg-
ment is there a trace of the real person. Burke was said to have
remarked on his "candour and lenity" and "his tenderness to the
subject" while Chesterfield said that "he discharged that duty in
a very different manner from most of his predecessors who were
too justly called the bloodhounds of the Crown."[7] However, his
strict interpretation of the most severe laws in defense of property
would lead the modern reader to regard this praise as a mere for-
mality.[8] His reluctance to assume the chancellorship in 1737 with-
out proper provision for his eldest son as Teller of the Exchequer
and the enormous increase in his own estate show clearly how mis-
placed was the poet's confidence that Hardwicke would be a bul-
wark against the power of accumulated wealth.[9]

It was certainly no tribute to his liberal views that Soame
Jenyns, rigorous defender of inherited wealth and social distinc-
tions, addressed several panegyrics to him, including a long imi-
tation of an epistle of Horace.[10] The separate praise to Hardwicke
published by George Lyttelton deserves more attention as coming
from a political figure who may have been the author of *Political
Justice*. In reply to eight lines of extemporaneous verse by Hard-
wicke, Lyttelton sent a lengthier verse letter to "Law's oracle,
the nation's pride."[11] His allegiance to Hardwicke was to grow

during the years.[12] Upon his retirement, in 1762, Lyttelton addressed a lengthy piece to him which included several passages that are similar in style and in occasional phrases to *Political Justice*.[13] It is true, however, that none of his earlier verses reaches its poetic merit save perhaps his "Verse to Mr. Glover on . . . Leonidas" (1734) or his six witty lines on Walpole's depriving Pitt of his commission in 1736, ending with "The service standard from thy freeborn hand / He took, and bade thee lead the patriot band." Two of Lyttelton's *Letters from a Persian* (1735) suggest the distinction drawn in the poem between law and justice (XII and XIIIL). Lyttelton's interest in Plato was to be demonstrated later in the *Dialogues of the Dead;* in the last dialogue, between Plato and Diogenes (added in 1765), contempt is cast on the "pageantry" inherent in monarchy, as in *Political Justice.*[14]

There are, however, strains in the poem which seem far removed from the general view of Lyttleton; this is especially true of the anti-monarchic and anti-property strictures, which remind one of the sentiments of the Commonwealth leveller, Gerard Winstanley.[15] The poem speaks of private property as fraudulent usurpation (14) and concludes with the orthodox advice to the rich as "Stewards to the Croud" to give fair and just "charities" (15). This position, however, is no different from Swift's in "On Mutual Subjection," a far from revolutionary statement on social and economic inequalities.[16] Occasional lines ring out with a strikingly unconventional force, such as those that imply an inalienable right to subsistence (14-16).[17] Similarly, the poet goes beyond Locke's easy acceptance of the original contract which established government: "In spite of Man's Consent, or Man's Decree, All have a Right to live, and to be free" (15). Certainly this can be declared a merely sentimental generalization like other commonplaces of the end of the century. There is, nevertheless a remarkable continuity of bitter aspersion on the bases of present society. For example, the king, that "necessary Curse of Heaven" (11), venerated simply for his "gorgeous Pomp" (13), is termed a (5). a "sceptered Slave," not "diff'rent from the Robber" (17-18). The power and property of the "lordling" entail "Want and Bondage on the World" or more properly on the "starv'd Peasant" (14). Strangely enough, commerce is presented favorably as an instrument to "make All, Fellow-citizens and Friends" (6). And of course Parliament, led by "these brave Youths" (22), can rehabilitate the nation.

We wonder at the motivation which will determine their salutary influence, since self-interest and every "private Claim" are decried as thoroughly as in Godwin's *Political Justice* of 1793 (5). It seems to lie in the "sacred flame of Social Love" (6 and 24), which by the primal factor of "equal Justice" (7) preaches universal benevolence. In this respect the poem follows Shaftesbury and, more particularly, Francis Hutcheson, who had been developing his concept of the innate moral sense during the previous decade. There is even a hint of the cause of the decline from the grace of impartial justice in the state of nature: since the advent of sin, "No more pure Reason earthly Minds can move" (11) and "Now began the Rage of wild Desire" (12). The veneration of calm reason that became the cult of the later revolutionary era serves here as well. Although there are formalized references to God as first cause (8-9) and to the Christian Faith (7), the poem is a strongly deistic statement. It has an unusual admixture of specifically Platonic ideas (9 and 12) and suggests some acquaintance with the Cambridge Platonists, who stressed the "inalienable value of reason as the last criterion of morality."[18] The "prebirth" strain is also strong in two effective passages (16 and 10).[19]

The clearest statements appealing for control of passion supply the most generally effective passages, far more intense in feeling and skillfully varied in style than the lengthy conclusion with its formalized tributes. An examination of these passages will support the view, we believe, that *Political Justice* rises above the level of the average political and occasional verse of the day. Of course it participates in the stock phrases and the tone of the standard couplet form without the consistent brilliance that the best works of Pope lent to it. But the influence of Pope is strong, as in "For this, let equal Justice rule the Ball!"[20] It may also be found in the unknown poet's fairly effective use of monosyllabic end rhymes.[21] The caesural pause is certainly rather too consistently, almost monotonously, placed after the fifth syllable, but effective variations can be found: "How fatal . . ." (5), "Heav'n throws . . ." (7), "Hence Reason . . ." (10), "Thus Pow'r . . ." (14). The poem, with few exceptions, uses the couplet as the unit of thought as well as of rhyme. Occasionally it has an aphoristic force that attests the skilled versifier: "Earth is their Parent; thither Kings should bend, / From her they rise, and not from Heav'n descend" (13). There are a fair number of effective antitheses emphasized shrewdly by alliterative touches: "Despotic Pow'r, and hoarded Heaps of Wealth, / Are forceful Robbery, and fraudful Stealth" (15). There are also some philosophic clichés: "Did the great System . . ." (8) and standard abstractions: "Corruption shall . . ." and "Dauntless . . ." (21).

By comparison with the vast body of the ephemeral verse of the day, however, this piece retains considerable vigor and grace. In the passages on justice, inalienable freedom, cloying luxury, and the engrossment of property it presages statements of Goldsmith in the "Deserted Village" (1770).[22] There are also several parallel passages in Burke's ironic *Vindication of Natural Society* (1756) relating to inborn ideas of justice, the abuses and complexity of the law, the opposition of natural to legal justice, the disproportion between a man's labors and his acquisitions, and the subversion of natural religion and human reason by "political laws."[23]

Burke's *Vindication* was acknowledged by Godwin as a source for his *Enquiry Concerning Political Justice.*[24] There may be a more direct link between these works of 1736 and 1793, however, than through Burke's satire or the growing criticism of unjust institutions of society. It is possible that Godwin saw the issue of the *Gentleman's Magazine* which reprinted *Fog's* review.[25] If so, We have an explanation for the similarity of the titles of both works, one with a mere hint of the anarchistic principle and the other comprising a complete, anti-government system. Whether or not the poem, *Political Justice,* was anything more than a transitory reflection of political history, for this, for its possible connections with Godwin, and for its intrinsic merits it has a claim upon our interests today.

Burton R. Pollin
The Bronx Community College
of the City University of New York
John Wilkes
New York University

NOTES

1. The American Philosophical Society, through a helpful grant given
   for another purpose, made possible the initial discovery at Yale.
   Acknowledgment should also be made of the aid of Mr. Richard Ban-
   croft of the British Museum in checking the provenance of its copy;
   similarly, of the aid of Barbara D. Simison of the Yale University
   Library. For the March publication date, see the *London Magazine*,
   V (March, 1736), 164 and the *Gentleman's Magazine*, VI (March, 1736),
   172, "Register of Books Published."

2. *The London Magazine*, V (April, 1736), 205; *Gentleman's Magazine*,
   VI (April, 1736), 210-211.

3. See Rose Mary Davis, *The Good Lord Lyttelton* (Bethlehem, Penn.,
   1939), pp. 45-46, 76.

4. Deism is once reprehended in this generally deistic poem (7), proba-
   bly as a term for atheism or Tindal's brand of religion; Woolston's
   Discourses on Miracles earned a severe sentence from Philip Yorke
   in 1728 according to George Harris, *Life of . . . Hardwicke* (London,
   1867), I, 205.

5. See Locke's *Second Treatise of Government*, Chapter V.

6. For an example of this widespread use of the corrpupt Spanish mon-
   archy see the *London Magazine*, V (June, 1736), 290-299, "Of the
   Declension and Destruction of Empires . . . ."

7. Harris, I, 237-238.

8. For cases during his administration of justice see P. C. Yorke, *Life
   and Correspondence of . . . Yorke* (Cambridge, 1913), I, 132-134,
   173-176.

9. York, I, 362-363.

10. See Jenyns, *Miscellaneous Pieces in Verse and Prose* (London,
    1793), I, 65-68 for the imitation of Epistle I of Book II, probably to
    be dated between 1735 and 1746 according to its placement; and
    imitations of Odes XVI of Book II and VIII of Book IV, pp. 103 and

109-113. The epistle of Horace, "Cum tot sustineas, et tanta negotia solus," may have influenced the tone and form of *Political Justice* as well.

11. Lyttleton, *Works* (London, 1776), III, 170-171.

12. R. M. Davis, 264; note also that in building his mansion, Hagley Hall, Lyttelton included a portrait of Hardwicke on the drawing room ceiling, pp. 257-258.

13. *Ibid.*, pp. 411-412; these were rescued from the Hardwicke MSS in the British Museum. Cf. "thy unbiast Mind, / Moved by no passions . . . ," "amidst the maze of Errors," and "seems / The arduous Temple's highest Steps to gain." Note also the absence of "hath" from all of Lyttelton's works and from *Political Justice*.

14. See Lyttelton, *Works,* III, 193-196, for "Verses to Mr. Glover"; III, 197, for his lines on Pitt; I, 165-166 for the two Letters; and II, 383-393 for the Dialogue. For Lyttelton's strong independence of mind and unconventional opinions in his *Observations on the Life of Cicero* (1733), see *SEL,* IV (Summer, 1964), 430-431.

15. For Winstanley's anomalous movement against private property and its complete failure and disappearance see David W. Petergorsky, *Left-Wing Democracy in the English Civil War* (London, 1940), pp. 180-183, 206, 230.

16. G. P. Gooch, *History of Democratic Ideas,* 2nd ed. (Cambridge, 1927), pp. 296-298, reports an undercurrent of anti-monarchic opinion about 1700 which soon vanished. The evidence of continuing radical doctrines in Augustan England given by Caroline Robbins in *The Eighteenth-Century Commonwealthman* (Cambridge, Mass., 1959), seems extremely inconclusive and minor.

17. Locke uses mankind's invention of money, rather ambiguously, to escape the implications of excessive engrossment, *op. cit.,* Ch. V.

18. Ernst Cassirer, *The Platonic Renaissance in England* (Austin, Texas, 1953), p. 84. Shaftesbury made the very pertinent ideas of Benjamin Whichcote's *Select Sermons* available for the next century in his 1698 edition. See his Aphorisms in the *Cambridge Platonists,* ed. E. T. Campagnac (Oxford, 1901), pp. xvi and 67.

19. The text (10, lower half) suggests Henry Vaughan's "The Retreat."

Silex Scintillans (1660 and 1665), was probably not known to the poet, but numerous contemporary works, such as Pope's *Essay on Criticism* (11.52-87) could provide related ideas and phrases.

20. Cf. Pope's "Elegy to an Unfortunate Lady," 1.35: "Thus, if Eternal justice rules the Ball."

21. Of 454 lines in the poem, 330 or 73% are monosyllabic in rhyme, while a random sampling of 100 lines from Pope's *Essay on Man* yields 85% — a significant but not major difference, if this technique is regarded as an aid to incisiveness and vigor.

22. See the entire sections from "Sweet smiling village" to "are no more" and from "Ye friends to truth" to "a garden and a grave" for comparison with "Take the starv'd Peasant's Taste . . ." (14) and "Such now thy State! . . ." (20). We mean simply that the mood of social criticism was slowly being generated by such statements, not that Goldsmith knew the poem directly.

23. *The Works of Burke* (Boston, 1806), I, 37-40, 43-44, 49-50.

24. Godwin's *Enquiry* 3rd ed. (London, 1798) I, 13, n.; 1st ed. (1793) also makes the acknowledgment.

25. In the Abinger MSS are notes made by Godwin in 1771 for a never-completed autobiography, referring to his reading back issues of the *Gentleman's Magazine*.

Political *JUSTICE.*

A

P O E M.

IN A

L E T T E R

TO THE

Right Hon. the Lord ****.

Juftum & tenacem propofiti virum,
Non civium ardor prava jubentium,
Non vultus inftantis tyranni
Mente quatit folida.   Hor.

L O N D O N:

Printed for J. Walthoe, over-againft the *Royal*
Exchange, in *Cornhill.*

M.DCC.XXXVI.

Political JUSTICE.

A

P O E M.

In a Letter *to the Right Hon. the Lord* * * * *.

WHILE You, my Lord, amidſt a *choſen Few*,
　　With *gen'rous Warmth* your *Country's Good* purſue;
While to that *Centre* all your *Wiſhes* tend;
Forgive th' officious Fondneſs of a Friend;
Anxious for You, who ſees with honeſt Dread
Thoſe Cliffs, that point the arduous Heights you tread;
Thoſe watchful Cares the ſlipp'ry Paths explore,
Where Thouſands fell of thoſe, who climb'd before.

　　LIKE your's, their Breaſts an hallow'd Spark inſpir'd;
But ſoon they blaz'd, by kindling Paſſion fir'd;

　　　　　　　　　　　　　　　　　Soon

Soon ruder Flames extinguiſh'd Reaſon's Light,
While Prejudices ſoul'd their jaundic'd Sight.

Such thro' falſe Optics ev'ry Object prove,
And try the Good and Bad by Hate and Love;
With all he wants, the favour'd Man ſupply,
And, to the hated, all he has deny.
Hence various Judgments forms the byas'd Throng,
Only alike in This, They all are wrong.

Would you, my Friend, not mix the purer Flame,
Nor ſink the Patriot in the baſeſt Name;
Nor factious Rage miſtake for public Zeal,
Nor partial Int'reſt for the gen'ral Weal;
Let calmer Reaſon uncontroul'd preſide,
And rig'rous Juſtice ev'ry Motion guide:
Plain are her Rules, and eaſy is her Way;
And yet how hard to find, if once you ſtray!
If once you careleſs leave the ſacred Ground,
Dark *Error* ſpreads its mazy Circle round:
Loſt and confounded, you ſhall blindly rove,
Still more bewilder'd ev'ry Step you move:
Horror and conſcious *Guilt* ſhall onward goad,
While *Habit* blunts the Thorns, and ſmooths the Road.

Ah!

A H ! never ftray, whatever End you gain ;
Tho' *Britain* perifh, or a C R O M W E L reign !
Tho' Heav'n's vaft Orbs be in Confufion hurl'd,
Juftice fhould triumph 'midft the fhatter'd World.

'T I S not enough you fcorn a *private* Claim,
And to your *Country's Good* direct your Aim ;
Wrong ftill is *Wrong*, however great the End ;
Tho' all the Realm were *Brother*, *Father*, *Friend* :
Juftice regards not thefe —— Where *Right* prevails,
A Nation's not an Atom in her Scales.
Act not for *Britain*, what you would defpife,
Tho' *Britain's* Sceptre were the tempting Prize.

H E only never errs, whofe Deeds are juft :
To this one Rule you may fecurely truft ;
Others may fail. If falfely underftood,
How fatal is the Thirft of public Good !
No heavier Curfe Almighty Vengeance brings,
Nor Plagues, nor Famine, nor the Luft of Kings.
Fir'd by this Rage, the phrentic Sons of *Rome*
The fuff'ring World to Death and Bondage doom :

B   Nations

Nations must sink, to raise her motley Frame;
And Millions bleed, to eternize her Name!
But, lo! her Glories fade! her Empire's past!
She madly conquers, but to fall the last!

Nor would I here, with narrow Views, reprove,
Or damp the sacred Flame of *Social Love*:
That saving Portion of th' Eternal Ray,
Sublimes our Souls, and animates our Clay;
Above low *Self* exalts our nobler Frame,
And emulates that *Heav'n*, from whence it came.
O would it never be confin'd to Place;
But beam, extensive, as the Human Race;
Be, as it was design'd, the World's great Soul,
Connect its Parts, and actuate the Whole;
Approach by Commerce Earth's remotest Ends,
And make All, Fellow-citizens and Friends!
Then Travellers from Pole to Pole might roam,
And shift their Climate, but not change their Home;
Each think himself a single Part alone,
And, for a Nation's Welfare, stake his own!
Yet, farther still, tho' dearest to the Breast,
That Nation think but part of all the rest!

For

FOR This, let equal *Juſtice* rule the Ball!
Her common Tie unites us all to all;
Of *Manners*, *Worſhip*, *Form*, no Diff'rence knows,
Condemns our *Friends*, and ſaves our *better Foes*.

ALL Ages this important Truth atteſt;
The *Man*, the *State*, that *juſtly* acts, is bleſt:
Guilt toils for Gain, at Honour's vaſt Expence;
Heav'n throws the Trifle in to Innocence;
And fixes Happineſs, in Hell's Deſpite,
The neceſſary Conſequence of Right.

THE *Juſt* are Heav'n's; and Earth's for Heav'n ordain'd,
Form'd by its Laws, and by its Laws maintain'd:
Theſe one true Int'reſt, one great Syſtem frame;
Political and *Moral* are the ſame.
Let ſubtle Guilt to Cunning lay Pretence;
The Man of Virtue is the Man of Senſe.
Proceed, ye Deiſts! blindfold Rage employ,
And prove the ſacred Truths ye would deſtroy;
Prove Chriſtian Faith the wiſeſt Rule to bind,
In Chains of cordial Love, our jarring Kind;

And

And thence conclude it human, if you can,
The perfect Produce of imperfect Man !
While we pronounce, the Author is Divine,
Whose simple Scheme can answer each Design ;
A Type of Heav'n make social Earth appear,
Where *Justice* tastes those Joys, that wait it there.

BUT *Int'rest* alters, and can never prove
A Rule, by which th' unvarying *Just* should move :
No Change revolving Time to *Justice* brings,
Fixt, as th' eternal Attributes of Things :
Older than Years, ere *Int'rest* had a Name,
Justice existed, and was still the same ;
In all his Works the great Creator's Guide ;
The Law, by which he form'd, by which he ty'd ;
By Reason's Light, not doubtful Words exprest ;
Stampt with his Image in the Creature's Breast.

BEFORE Creation was, th' Almighty Mind,
From long Eternity, the World design'd ;
Did the great System in its Parts survey,
And fit the Springs, and regulate their Play ;
In meet Gradations plan th' harmonious Round,
Those Links, by which depending Parts are bound :

All

All thefe he faw, ere yet the Things he made,
In Types, which well the mimic World difplay'd;
Thefe Types are real, fince from them he drew
The real Forms of whatfoe'er we view.
Made to their Semblance Heav'n and Earth exift;
But they unmade eternally fubfift;
For if created, we muft fure fuppofe
Some other Types, whence their Refemblance flows;
While thefe on others equally depend,
Nor ever fhall the long Progreffion end.
God, ere he acts, the future Being fees,
Or does he knows not what, by blind Decrees;
And Chance could never frame the vaft Defign,
Where countlefs Parts in jufteft Order join.

THE Types eternal all Proportions teach,
Greater or lefs, more or lefs perfect each:
Nor thefe with empty Forms the Mind employ,
Which Thought at Will can raife, at Will deftroy.
One Foot exceeds its Half, and Pow'r divine
Could never change the Nature of that Line.
Angels than *Men* more perfect Beings are,
And more Perfections *Men* than *Beafts* declare.

C

Thefe

These Truths eternal *Pow'r* Omniscient sees;
On these he forms his ever-made Decrees:
Nor can he better love what merits least,
Man than an *Angel,* or than *Man a Beast:*
Hence *Reason* hence immortal *Order* springs:
Knowledge and *Love,* that justly suit the *Things;*
And thence th'unerring Rule of *Justice* flows,
To act as *Order* prompts, and *Reason* shows.

WHEN *Man* in Nature's Purity remain'd,
By Pain untroubled, and by Sin unstain'd,
Fair Image of the God; and closely join'd
By Inmate Union to the heav'nly Mind;
In the pure Splendor of substantial Light,
The Beam divine of Reason blest his Sight;
Seraphic Order in its Charms he view'd;
Seeing, he lov'd; and loving, he pursu'd:
Nor dar'd the Body, passive Slave, controul
The sov'reign Mandates of the ruling Soul.

BUT soon by Sin the sacred Union broke,
Man bows to Earth beneath the heavy Yoke;
The darkling Soul scarce feels a glimm'ring Ray,
Shut in gross Sense from out immortal Day.

Now

Now righteous Vengeance injur'd Order arms,
And wraps in Terrors its celeftial Charms.
Material Objects Heav'n-born Souls poffefs;
Paffions inflave, and fervile Cares opprefs:
Fraud, Rapine, Murder, Guilt's long direful Crew,
Diftracted Nature's Anarchy purfue.
No more pure Reafon earthly Minds can move;
No more can Order's Charms perfuafive prove:
But as the Moon, reflecting borrow'd Day,
Sheds on our fhadow'd World a feeble Ray;
Some fcatter'd Beams of Reafon Law contains;
While Order's Rule muft be inforc'd by Pains:
Hence written Statutes, Tortures hence are giv'n,
And *K —gs*, the neceffary Curfe of Heav'n.
Tho' Nature had not form'd the fubject Ball
For *Man* alone, a Being rais'd o'er all;
Yet fome Things were for human Ufe defign'd;
And thefe in common dealt to human Kind;
Still to our Wants is giv'n a Pow'r to ufe,
What Heav'n to our Perfections might refufe.
This faithful Inftinct in each Breaft implants;
All know their Rights, for all muft feel their Wants.

BUT

BUT now began the Rage of wild Defire
To thirſt for more than Uſe could e'er require ;
One on another prey'd ; thence Jars aroſe,
Till juſt Partitions could their Heats compoſe.
Yet ſtill th'unvary'd Claim of each remain'd ;
The Right is gen'ral, tho' the Uſe reſtrain'd ;
Nor could th'invalid Act of *Man* deſtroy
What Nature made, and gave him to enjoy.

AND now ſome Sages, high by others deem'd,
For Virtue honour'd, and for Parts eſteem'd ;
Impow'r'd by All, impartially preſide,
Determine Bounds, when dubious Claims are try'd ;
Direct with prudent Rules the various Throng ;
And mark the *Right* diſtinctly from the *Wrong*.
The ſimple Precept ſubtle Wiles evade,
And Statutes, as our Crimes increas'd, are made :
Theſe were at firſt unwritten, plain, and few ;
Till ſwell'd by Time the Law's vaſt Volume grew :
And Sages then, however wiſe and juſt,
Were found unequal to th'unweildy *Truſt* :
Others o'er them were plac'd, ſtill more o'er theſe ;
Thus *Government* grew up by ſlow Degrees :

Higher

Higher the Pile arofe, and ftill more high,
When, lo! the Summit ends in *Monarchy*.
There plac'd, a Man in gorgeous Pomp appears,
And far o'er Earth his tow'ring Afpect rears;
While proftrate Crowds his facred Smiles implore,
And what their Crimes had form'd, their Fears adore.
Low from beneath they lift their fervile Eyes,
And fee the proud *Coloffus* touch the Skies.
At fome high Mountain's Foot when Children gaze,
They think the Top their Heads to Heav'n would raife;
But when they mount, their Wonder ftill is more,
That the blue Arch feems diftant as before.
So views the Crowd a Throne; but Thofe, who rife,
Can claim no nearer Kindred to the Skies:
Earth is their *Parent ;* thither *Kings* fhould bend;
From her they rife, and not from Heav'n defcend.

So *Pow'r* fupreme thro' diff'rent Stages rofe;
While *Property* in like Proportion grows:
By *Induftry* One gains his Neighbour's Share,
And leaves the Whole to his acquiring Heir;
Till various Parts compofe the vaft Eftate,
And Numbers ftarve to make one *Lordling* great:

D   Thus

Thus *Pow'r*, with *Property* abus'd, prevails ;
And *Want* and *Bondage* on the World intails.
Tho' such the *Steps*, by which the *Great* aspire ;
Tho' such the *Means*, by which the *Rich* acquire:
None better can suppose, some point out worse :
Riches by *Fraud*, and *Pow'r* by lawless *Force*!
Yet ev'n in *such* what Title can they find,
T'engross the *Properties* of human Kind ?
Can *Man*, by Nature free, by Nature made
To share the Feast her bounteous Hand display'd,
Transfer these *Rights* ? As well he may dispense
With those he boasts to *Reason* and to *Sense* :
While, like blind *Indians*, Others would enjoy
The native Gifts of *Wretches* they destroy.

TAKE the starv'd *Peasant's Taste*, devouring *Lord*,
Ere you deprive him of the genial *Board* ;
And if you would his *Liberty* controul,
First curb the various Actings of his *Soul*.

BUT yet admit the Sire his *Right* foregoes ;
Can he his Childrens sep'rate *Claim* dispose ?
No, tho' he should resume whate'er he gave,
He cannot take what they from *Nature* have ;

And,

And, fpite of Man's Confent, or Man's Decree,
All have a Right to live, and to be free.

Ye Gods of Earth, how vainly are ye proud
Of Things, which make ye Stewards to the Croud!
When wide's your Sway, when large your treafur'd Store,
They but increafe your Servitude the more:
A Part is only yours, the reft is theirs;
And nothing all your own, except your Cares:
Then how muft your Account, rafh Wafters! end,
Whofe *All*'s fo little, yet who *Millions* fpend?
Whofe greateft *Charities* are barely *juft*,
Whofe *righteous Rule*'s a mere Difcharge of *Truft*.
Defpotic Pow'r, and hoarded Heaps of Wealth,
Are forceful Robbery, and fraudful Stealth.

Yet Magiftrates muft rule; they're ufeful Things;
Our Guilt the Vengeance, and th'Avenger brings.

Such now is Man deprav'd, that *Fear* muft fway
To tread thofe Paths, where *Duty* points the Way:
The *Wretch* muft fuffer, to forewarn the *reft*;
And *Some* muft fall, to ftop the fpreading *Peft*.

Hence

Hence *Public Pains :* What to the Crime is due,
O Judge Supreme ! muft be referv'd to You.
Alone the *gen'ral Welfare* can demand
The bleeding Victim from th'unwilling Hand.

THIS well *You* know, O * YORK ! whofe *righteous* Seat
Gives to the *Innocent* a fure Retreat :
Severely juft, and pioufly fevere,
The *Crime* you punifh, while the *Pain* you fhare :
Tears, with the dreadful Words of Sentence, flow ;
Nor can the rigid *Judge* the *Man* forego.

FAR other He ; (blufh, *Nature !* fuch there are,)
Whom *Agony* can feaft, and *Groans* can chear ;
With gloomy Joy elate, whofe baleful Breath,
Triumphant, fwells with the dread Sounds of *Death* ;
Who on th'imploring Face, malignant, fmiles ;
And fentenc'd Wretches wantonly reviles.

THO', for Convenience fram'd, the *Laws* fhould fhine,
Pure Emanation from the Source Divine !
Such as can pierce the Gloom of *Pagan* Night,
And untaught *Savages* in Woods inlight ;

* Lord HARDWICK.

Such

As can the *Murd'rer's* lifted Arm arreft,
And blaft the Crime within the *Traitor's* Breaft.
Such as th'offending Wretch, indignant, owns,
And hails its Beauty with his dying Groans;
Such as, on *Scaffolds*, can the *Guiltlefs* fave;
And torture on his *Throne*, the *Sceptred Slave*.

IN fuch fair Laws the Will of Heav'n Impreft,
Shines to all Eyes, and rules the confcious Breaft:
Tho' Tortures fleep, tho' Night's thick mantling Veil
From mortal Ken the fecret Deed conceal;
Nature and *Confcience* fhall awake within,
And light the Shade, and loud proclaim the Sin.
But *Laws*, which fpring from the polluted Source
Of Human Paffion, urg'd by favage Force,
Whate'er their Pow'r, whate'er their Influence be,
Can never bind the Man, by Nature free!
Man, by no Rule, by no one Pow'r confin'd;
Save where juft Order, and fair Reafon's join'd!

THO' fwaying Might conftrains the mortal Frame,
The free-born Soul afferts her native Claim;
Nor can confound, to pleafe a Tyrant's Luft,
Th'eternal Barriers, fixt, of Wrong and Juft.

E

Tho' proud Oppreſſion boaſt a ſov'reign Court,
Yet Heav'n's Tribunal is the laſt Reſort :
There ſuff'ring Innocence finds quick Redreſs ;
And *Juſtice* damns, who legally oppreſs.

But ſhould the univerſal Voice agree
To hail an Act of legal *Tyranny* ;
Can the vain Breath of an inconſtant Throng
Make an Act *right*, which is by Nature *wrong* ?
And, changing thus of Things th'unvary'd Courſe,
What in itſelf can never bind, inforce ?
Firſt let their Breath diveſt the Day of Light ;
To blazon forth the dusky Face of Night !
Can human Will ſubvert what was deſign'd,
Decreed, and will'd by the All-ruling Mind ?
Muſt not thoſe Bounds all human Pow'r confine ?
The utmoſt Limits ev'n of Pow'r divine !
That Source ! from whence all lawful Rule muſt ſpring ;
And diff'rent from the *Robber* marks the *King* !

The Prince, who thus perverts Imperial Sway ;
Tho' willing Slaves implicitly obey ;

Tho',

Tho', by a long Defcent from *Adam* down,
Succeffive Rule confirms his lawful Crown;
As Nature's Rebel, forfeits ev'ry Claim,
And loads the *Tyrant* with th'*Ufurper*'s Name;
While with each lawlefs Act of high Command,
He ftands profcrib'd by his own guilty Hand.

WHAT then were you, O * CHARLES! whofe Sires by
Were rais'd; the Monarchs of a People's Voice?
[Choice
Their Gift your Sceptre, and their Good alone,
The End, the Bafis, that fuftain'd your Throne!
No longer could your Right to rule extend,
Than while your duteous Care preferv'd the End.
Yet you by Bribes a venal Herd imploy'd,
And ftripp'd *Caftile* with her own Wealth deftroy'd;
While Thefe, a few, fafely intrench'd in Laws
Made to fecure fair *Freedom*'s glorious Caufe,
The facred Means to flavifh Ends apply'd,
And *Freedom* with the Bands of *Juftice* ty'd.
Should bleeding *Spain* her *Spoiler*'s Pow'r endure,
Becaufe black *Fraud* and *Treachery* fecure?

* CHARLES V. Emperor and King of *Spain.*

O

Should you deſtroy her, while your Reign prepares
Her Children's Plunder for your future Heirs ;
And Both the moſt accurſt of Mortals leaves,
Your own all *Tyrants*, and her Race all *Slaves !*
Vainly you ſeek in Shades a quiet Mind,
And caſt the Load of *Government* behind
Your former Crimes the Solitude invade ;
Yourſelf the laſt poor Wretch your Pow'r has made.

Now, loſt *Iberia !* Rapine holds the Reins,
And loads thy groaning Sons with galling Chains !
Theſe were the Steps by which tyrannic Might
Roſe from the Shade of Guilt's tremendous Night ;
Advanc'd by ſlow Degrees its Giant Size,
Tow'r'd o'er thy Realms, and proudly brav'd the Skies :
Stalk'd waſteful on, and ſhook the flaming Rod,
While dire Deſtruction mark'd where'er it trod ;
While trampled Liberty in vain implor'd,
And grov'ling Slaves the Royal Fiend ador'd.

Such now thy State ! ah ! how unlike thoſe Reigns,
When genial Freedom brooded o'er thy Plains ?
The Rich in Peace their plenteous Stores enjoy'd,
By Cares unvext, by Luxury uncloy'd :

Hope

Hope chear'd the Poor with Promises of Gain;
And paid, with future Joys, their present Pain;
Shew'd the full Bowl amidst their sultry Toil;
While Those, who prun'd the Olive, drank the Oil:
By Night of all the Fruits of Day possest,
Labour weigh'd down the Eye, and sweeten'd Rest.
Such was thy State, when blest with *Freedom*'s Smiles;
And such is now the State of *Britain*'s Isles.
Long may the Treasure to her Sons descend!
What *Virtue* gain'd, may *Virtue* still defend!
O glorious *Spirit*! never may you cease;
But, as you blaz'd in *War*, shine forth in *Peace*!
Dauntless, with all the Force of Truth engage
The headlong Tide of each corrupted Age!
Tho' not a Foe appears, be still prepar'd;
And, tho' no Danger threatens, keep your Guard!
Should you once droop, and close your watchful Eyes,
Never again shall you attempt to rise;
Corruption shall a deadly Spell dispense,
Unnerve your Pow'rs, and stupify your Sense:
So shall you lie in Golden Fetters bound,
Till ruder Chains shall fix you to the Ground:
Wake then, and ease the Weight of *Britain*'s Throne;
Nor let our mighty MONARCH wake alone.

WHILE

WHILE *Greece* and *Rome* record an hoary Train,
Who dar'd the Cause of *Liberty* maintain:
The *British* Senate boasts a youthful Band,
Form'd for th'exalted Task by *Nature's* Hand:
She gave their Souls with early Charms to shine,
And Love of Arts, these Beauties to refine:
She gave those Thoughts, which she alone inspires,
And deck'd them out in all that Care acquires;
Wisdom, unclogg'd by Years, by Pain unbought;
A Zeal by Vigour kindled, rul'd by Thought;
Such Gifts she to her favour'd Sons imparts;
To judging Heads, and to determin'd Hearts;
To *Heads* unfir'd by *Youth's* tumultuous Rage,
To *Hearts* unnumb'd by the chill Ice of *Age*:
Yet, while they both preserve a sep'rate Claim,
Their *Passions reason*, and their *Reasons flame*.

IN these brave Youths no Luxury implants
The real Poorness of phantastic Wants;
Nor to Temptations are their Hearts betray'd,
To fill Desires, which *Nature* never made.
To them one Dish, with some dear Friend to taste,
Were better than TRIMALCHIO's crouded Feast;

Better

Better in homefpun Beds at Eafe to lie,
Than prefs the *Tyrian* Couch with fleeplefs Eye ;
So to enjoy the paft in Golden Dreams,
Or plan for *Britain*'s Good fome future Schemes,
Can *Thefe* a Joy in *gilded Chariots* find,
Who know the Tranfports of an *honeft Mind*?
Who, fhould they walk along the public Way,
Hear grateful Crouds their Adorations pay.

Loll then, ye Great, fupinely in your Cars ;
Stop ev'ry Paffage to your confcious Ears ;
Shut out the Woes ye caufe, the bitter Cries
Of Thofe, who call down Vengeance from the Skies.
While you, brave Patriots ! from each Tongue receive
A glorious Tribute for the Joys you give !
While all the *Good* your deathlefs Praife proclaim ;
And, higher Praife ! while all the *Bad* defame ;
Be this your Pride ! In Youth's unfully'd Minds
Her fitteft Manfion heav'nly *Virtue* finds.

And You, my Friend ! who fill the foremoft Place,
The godlike Cato of the youthful Race ;
While fome in hoftile Fields deferve Renown,
Theirs be the Laurel, your's the Olive Crown !

For.

For, truft to Fame, thofe Heroes brighter fhone,
Who *fav'd* a Nation, than who Nations *won*.

SUCH be thy Guides, whofe great Examples prove,
That *Juftice* fans the Flame of *Social Love*.

F I N I S.

ERRATUM.
Page 3, Line 7, for *Theſe* read *Whoſe*.

THE AUGUSTAN REPRINT SOCIETY

WILLIAM ANDREWS CLARK MEMORIAL LIBRARY
University of California, Los Angeles

PUBLICATIONS IN PRINT

1948-1949

16. Nevil Payne, *Fatal Jealousy* (1673).
17. Nicholas Rowe, *Some Account of the Life of Mr. William Shakespeare* (1709).
18. "Of Genius," in *The Occasional Paper*, Vol. III, No. 10 (1719); and Aaron Hill's Preface to *The Creation* (1720).

1949-1950

22. Samuel Johnson, *The Vanity of Human Wishes* (1749) and two *Rambler* papers (1750)
23. John Dryden, *His Majesties Declaration Defended* (1681).

1950-1951

26. Charles Macklin, *The Man of the World* (1792).

1951-1952

31. Thomas Gray, *An Elegy Wrote in a Country Churchyard* (1751); and *The Eton College Manuscript.*

1952-1953

41. Bernard Mandeville, *A Letter to Dion* (1732).

1954-1955

49. Two St. Cecilia's Day Sermons (1696, 1697).
52. Pappity Stampoy, *A Collection of Scotch Proverbs* (1663).

1958-1959

75. John Joyne, *A Journal* (1679).
76. André Dacier, *Preface to Aristotle's Art of Poetry* (1705).

1959-1960

80. [P. Whalley], *An Essay on the Manner of Writing History* (1746).
83. *Sawney and Colley* (1742) and other Pope Pamphlets.
84. Richard Savage, *An Author to be lett* (1729).

1960-1961

85-6. *Essays on the Theatre from Eighteenth-Century Periodicals.*
90. Henry Needler, *Works* (1728).

1961-1962

93. John Norris, *Cursory Reflections Upon a Book Call'd, An Essay Concerning Human Understanding* (1690).
94. An. Collins, *Divine Songs and Meditacions* (1653).
95. *An Essay on the New Species of Writing Founded by Mr. Fielding* (1751).
96. *Hanoverian Ballads.*

1962-1963

97. Myles Davies, Selections from *Athenae Britannicae* (1716-1719).
98. *Select Hymns Taken Out of Mr. Herbert's Temple* (1697).
99. Thomas Augustine Arne, *Artaxerxes* (1761).
100. Simon Patrick, *A Brief Account of the New Sect of Latitude Men* (1662).
101-2. Richard Hurd, *Letters on Chivalry and Romance* (1762).

1963-1964

103. Samuel Richardson, *Clarissa*: Preface, Hints of Prefaces, and Postscript.
104. Thomas D'Urfey, *Wonders in the Sun, or, the Kingdom of the Birds* (1706).
105. Bernard Mandeville, *An Enquiry into the Causes of the Frequent Executions at Tyburn* (1725).
106. Daniel Defoe, *A Brief History of the Poor Palatine Refugees* (1709).
107-8. John Oldmixon, *An Essay on Criticism* (1728).

William Andrews Clark Memorial Library: University of California, Los Angeles

THE AUGUSTAN REPRINT SOCIETY

GENERAL EDITORS

EARL MINER
University of California, Los Angeles

MAXIMILLIAN E. NOVAK
University of California, Los Angeles

LAWRENCE CLARK POWELL
Wm. Andrews Clark Memorial Library

Corresponding Secretary: Mrs. Edna C. Davis, Wm. Andrews Clark Memorial Library

The Society's purpose is to publish reprints (usually facsimile reproductions) of rare seventeenth and eighteenth century works. All income of the Society is devoted to defraying costs of publication and mailing.

Correspondence concerning subscriptions in the United States and Canada should be addressed to the William Andrews Clark Memorial Library, 2205 West Adams Boulevard, Los Angeles, California. Correspondence concerning editorial matters may be addressed to any of the general editors. The membership fee is $5.00 a year for subscribers in the United States and Canada and 30/- for subscribers in Great Britain and Europe. British and European subscribers should address B. H. Blackwell, Broad Street, Oxford, England. Copies of back issues in print may be obtained from the Corresponding Secretary.

PUBLICATIONS FOR 1964-1965

JOHN TUTCHIN, *Selected Poems* (1685-1700). Introduction by Spiro Peterson.

SIR WILLIAM TEMPLE, *An Essay upon the Original and Nature of Government* (1680). Introduction by Robert C. Steensma.

T. R., *An Essay Concerning Critical and Curious Learning* (1698). Introduction by Curt A. Zimansky.

ANONYMOUS, *Political Justice. A Poem* (1736). Introduction by Burton R. Pollin and John W. Wilkes.

Two Poems Against Pope: LEONARD WELSTED, *One Epistle to Mr. A. Pope* (1730); ANONYMOUS, *The Blatant Beast* (1740). Introduction by Joseph V. Guerinot.

ROBERT DODSLEY, *An Essay on Fable* (1764). Introduction by Jeanne K. Welcher and Richard Dircks.

THE AUGUSTAN REPRINT SOCIETY

William Andrews Clark Memorial Library

2205 WEST ADAMS BOULEVARD, LOS ANGELES, CALIFORNIA 90018

Make check or money order payable to THE REGENTS OF THE UNIVERSITY OF CALIFORNIA.